THE
Big Book
OF
Games
Dorothy Stott

Dutton Children's Books

New York

Text copyright © 1998 by Dutton Children's Books
Illustrations copyright © 1998 by Dorothy Stott
Games compiled and written by Susan Van Metre

Library of Congress Cataloging-in-Publication Data
Stott, Dorothy M. The big book of games / by Dorothy Stott.
—1st ed.   p. cm. Includes index. Summary: Provides directions
for playing a variety of indoor and outdoor games, party games,
car games, and singing games. ISBN 0-525-45454-3 1. Games—
Juvenile literature. [1. Games.] I. Title. GV1203.S77
1998 790.1'922—dc21 96-53674 CIP AC

Published in the United States 1998 by
Dutton Children's Books, a division of Penguin Putnam Books for Young Readers,
375 Hudson Street, New York, New York 10014

Designed by Adrian Leichter
Printed in Italy
First Edition
1 3 5 7 9 10 8 6 4 2

The publisher gratefully acknowledges permission to
reprint "I'm a Little Teapot," written by Clarence Kelley and
George Sanders. Copyright © 1939 Kelman Music Corporation.
Copyright renewed 1967 by Marilyn Sanders O'Bradovich.
International Copyright Secured. All rights reserved.

FOR DANA WITHERELL

You are missed.

Contents

Choosing Who Is IT or Who Goes First

To begin playing many of the games in this book, you and your friends will need to choose one of the group to be *It*. *It* has to do something different from the rest of the group, like searching when everyone else is hiding, or chasing when everyone else is running.

In other games, like Hopscotch and Horse, you need to choose a player to go first. Often, more than one person will want to be *It* or to go first. Here are some fair ways to choose one person for these roles. (If you need to decide who will go second, third, and so on, you can also use any of these methods to determine the order of the other players.)

● Eeny, Meeny, Miny, Mo

Everyone stands in a circle, and one player chants the following rhyme. As she says each word, she points to each player in turn, including herself. Whoever she is pointing at when she says the last word of the rhyme is *It* or goes first in the game.

Eeny, meeny, miny, mo,
Catch a tiger by the toe.
If he hollers, let him go,
Eeny, meeny, miny, mo.

One Potato, Two Potato

All the players stand in a circle with one fist extended in front of them. One player touches each fist in turn, including his own, as he chants the following rhyme:

> *One potato, two potato,*
> *Three potato, four.*
> *Five potato, six potato,*
> *Seven potato, more.*
> *Y-O-U spells you and O-U-T spells out.*

The person he touches when he says "out" must put her fist behind her back. Then he keeps repeating the rhyme and touching fists until only one person has a fist in front of him. This person is *It* or goes first.

Rock, Paper, Scissors

On the count of three, each player in the group puts one hand out, shaped like either:

a rock,　　　　　　　*a piece of paper,*　　　　　　*or a pair of scissors*

Rock beats scissors, scissors beat paper, and paper beats rock. If the symbol you make is beaten by another player's symbol, then you are out. Keep playing until just one person is left. This person is *It* or goes first.

Flipping a Coin

If there are only two players in your game, you can flip a coin (or a milk cap) to decide who goes first. While one player tosses a coin in the air, the other player calls "heads" or "tails." If the coin lands on the side he guessed, he goes first. If it doesn't, the player who tossed the coin goes first.

Choosing Teams

To play some of the games in this book, players must be divided into teams. The easiest way to choose teams is to have everyone line up and count off. The first player in line says "one," the second says "two," and so on. Everyone with an even number is on one team, and those with an odd number are on the other.

Outdoor Games

9

KICK THE CAN

WHAT YOU NEED

- *4 or more players*
- *a can or plastic bottle*
- *a large area or blocked-off street surrounded by good hiding places*

**This game is noisy and fast.
It's great to play with lots of friends.**

1 Place the can in a marked spot. Pick another area to be the jail.

2 Choose someone to be *It*. (See page 6.)

3 Another player, someone with a strong foot, kicks the can as hard as she can. *It* retrieves the can and returns it to the marked area while all the other players run and hide.

4 *It* closes her eyes and counts to ten. Then she opens them and starts looking for the other players.

5 When *It* sees someone, she calls out the player's name and hiding place. *It* and the player must then race each other back to the can to see who can kick it first.

10

6 If *It* kicks the can first, the player goes to jail and stays there until another player frees him.

7 If the player kicks the can first, he and any players already in jail are free to hide again, and *It* must retrieve the can before hunting for them.

8 Players do not have to wait until *It* spots them to run and kick the can. They can sneak up and kick the can anytime to free friends from jail, so *It* should try to keep an eye on the can while hunting.

9 The game ends when *It* puts everyone in jail.

● **Helpful hint:** If there are a lot of players, it may be too difficult for *It* to put everyone in jail at once, so you may want to set a time limit, such as twenty minutes, after which *It* can choose someone else to be *It*.

SPUD

**This game has a funny name
that is another word for *potato*. Perhaps
it used to be played with a potato
instead of a ball.**

1 Choose someone to be *It*. (See page 6.)

2 *It* gives each player a different number.

3 Then *It* throws the ball high into the air and calls out the number of one of the players. This player must run and catch the ball while all of the other players, including *It*, try to run as far away from the ball as possible.

4 When the designated player has retrieved the ball, he calls out "SPUD!" and all the other players must freeze where they are.

- *4 or more players*
- *a large rubber ball*
- *a large area*

5 The player with the ball takes four steps toward the closest player, spelling out "S-P-U-D" as he walks. None of the other players is allowed to move.

6 When he has finished walking, the player throws the ball at the closest person. If he hits her, she gets the letter "S" and is *It*. If he misses, he gets the letter and is *It*. When someone gets all of the letters in "SPUD," he is out of the game.

7 The game is over when all but one player, the winner, is out.

● **For more fun:** The person who is *It* can also call out a number that doesn't belong to anyone when he throws the ball. Then he catches the ball himself and calls out "SPUD!"

13

DODGEBALL

- *6 or more players*
- *a piece of chalk*
- *a large rubber ball*
- *a large area*

You have to be quick to play this game, because if the ball hits you, you're out.

1 Draw a very large chalk circle, big enough for several players to run around in.

2 Divide the group into two teams. (See page 8.)

3 One team stands inside the circle; the other team stands outside of it.

4 The players on the outside take turns throwing the ball at the legs of the players inside the circle. The outside team cannot step inside the circle unless they are retrieving the ball.

5 The players inside the circle try to move away from the ball without stepping out-of-bounds. If a player is hit with the ball, she joins the players outside the circle.

6 When there is only one player left in the circle, she is the winner for her team.

7 The teams can now switch places and play again.

● **Safety tip:** Do not throw the ball at anyone's stomach or head—that hurts!

14

keepaway

This simple game is one you may already have played, particularly if you have a pesky younger brother or sister!

1 Choose two people to be ball throwers.

2 The rest of the players stand between them.

3 The ball throwers toss the ball back and forth, trying to keep the other players from catching it.

4 If a player in the middle catches the ball, he gets to be one of the ball throwers, replacing whoever threw the ball to him.

● **Helpful hint:** This game can go on forever! Play as long as it's fun for everyone.

15

HOPSCOTCH

WHAT YOU NEED

- *2 or more players*
- *chalk*
- *1 pebble for each player*
- *a smooth area like a driveway or sidewalk*

Children all over the world, from Charleston to China, test their hopping and balancing skills by playing a version of this game.

1 With the chalk, draw a Hopscotch course made up of ten numbered boxes. It could look like this [**A**] or this [**B**], or you can make up your own design.

2 Choose a player to go first. (See page 6.) This player tosses his pebble into the first box. If he misses, the next player takes a turn. If the pebble lands in the box, the player can now hop on one foot from box to box, being sure not to step on a line, and avoiding the box with his pebble in it. (If two boxes are side by side, the player can land on two feet with one foot in each box.)

3 When he has reached the last box, he hops back from box to box in reverse order. When he gets back to the square with his pebble in it, he must bend over, while still on one foot, and pick up the pebble before he finishes hopping.

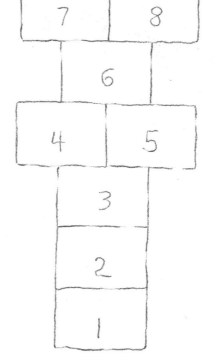

A

B

4 If the first player successfully hops the course and picks up his pebble, he gets to try to land his pebble in the second box and hop the course again.

5 Whenever a player makes a mistake, he leaves his pebble in the last box he tossed it into and lets the next player take a turn. As this player hops through the course, she must avoid the box with the first player's pebble in it, as well as the one with her own pebble.

6 The first player to land his pebble in the tenth box and hop through the entire course wins.

● **For more fun:** If you step on a line or hop in a box with a pebble in it, but none of the other players notice, then you can yell "Butterfingers!" and keep hopping.

Jacks

Jacks is a fun game you can play almost anywhere—by yourself or with friends.

- *1 or more players*
- *a small rubber ball*
- *10 jacks*
- *a flat area*

1 Hold all the jacks in one hand. Drop them gently onto a flat surface so that they land about an inch apart.

2 Bounce the rubber ball close to the jacks. The higher you bounce it, the more time you have to pick up the jacks!

3 While the ball is in the air, pick up one jack.

4 Then hurry to catch the ball before it hits the ground. Put the jack aside.

5 Bounce the ball again and repeat the "one jack pickup" for the other nine jacks, putting each one aside after you have picked it up. This is called "one-sies." Be sure not to knock any of the other jacks as you pick each one up, or you lose your turn.

6 Two-sies is just like one-sies, except now you pick up two jacks at a time.

1

2

18

7 After you have picked up all the jacks in pairs, you move on to three at a time, four at a time, and so on, until you can pick up *all ten* jacks in one big scoop. On certain sets, such as three-sies, four-sies, six-sies, etc., you will have leftover jacks. You should scoop them up, too, before going on to the next set.

8 If you drop one of the jacks, or if you don't catch the ball before it hits the ground, it is the next player's turn.

9 If you are playing by yourself or if you get another turn, start with the number of jacks you were picking up when you made your mistake.

10 The first person to successfully scoop up all ten jacks is the winner!

● **Helpful hint:** Don't scrape your knuckles on the sidewalk when you are scooping!

MaRBLeS

Children in early Rome played a similar game with nuts instead of marbles. Marbles are easier to roll!

- *2 or more players*
- *chalk*
- *an equal number of marbles (5–10) for each player*
- *a large marble, or shooter, for each player*

1 Draw a three-foot-wide circle with your piece of chalk.

2 Each player chooses one large marble to use as a shooter and places the rest of his or her marbles inside the circle.

3 Choose a player to go first. (See page 6.) The first player places his shooter on the edge of the circle and flicks it hard with his thumb at the marbles inside. He tries to knock a marble out of the circle.

20

4 If he succeeds and his shooter stays inside the circle, he gets another turn, shooting from wherever his shooter stopped rolling. He gets to keep each marble he knocks out. If his shooter rolls outside the circle or he doesn't knock another marble out, then it is the next player's turn.

5 The game is over when all the marbles have been knocked out of the circle. The player with the most marbles wins.

● **For more fun:** To make the game a little more challenging, you can arrange the marbles inside the circle in a cross shape like this [**A**], a circle like this [**B**], or in a pile.

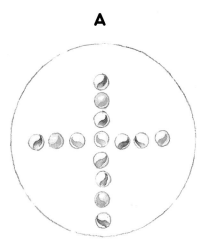

A

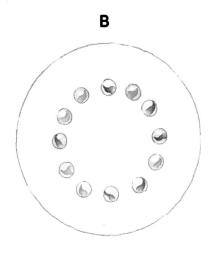

B

21

- *4 or more players*
- *a large, clear area*

MOTHER, MAY I?

This game gives you a chance to play the parent, but pay attention! Don't let your "kids" do anything without your permission!

1 Choose someone to be Mother, or *It*. (See page 6.)

2 The players line up about twenty-five feet away from Mother.

3 Now Mother tells each player how many steps he may take toward her (usually three or four). She tells them what kind of steps, too:

BABY STEPS:
Tiny steps with one foot right in front of the other

LEAPING STEPS:
Hopping steps

SCISSOR STEPS:
Sideways steps with one leg crossing over the other

GIANT STEPS:
The biggest steps that you can take

BANANA STEPS:
Cartwheels

4 But before they can move, the players must remember to ask, "Mother, may I?" When Mother says, "Yes, you may," the player gets to move forward.

5 But if the player forgets to ask permission, then he loses a turn.

6 Mother keeps giving instructions until one player is close enough to touch her. This player is the winner and gets to be Mother in the next game.

ReD LIGHT, GReeN LIGHT

Like cars on the road, you can move only
when the stoplight is green for GO.

WHAT YOU NEED

- 4 or more players
- chalk
- a large, flat area

1 Use the chalk to draw a starting line long enough for several players to stand behind.

2 Choose someone to be *It*. (See page 6.)

3 The players stand behind the starting line facing *It*, who stands about twenty-five feet away.

4 *It* turns her back to the players and says "Green light!" Now all the players run toward her as fast as they can.

5 But as soon as *It* says "Red light!" and turns around, all of the players must stop.

6 If *It* sees any player still moving when she turns around, she tells the player to go back to the starting line.

7 The game continues until someone tags *It*. This player is the winner and gets to be *It* in the next game.

JUMP ROPE

- *3 or more players*
- *a jump rope*
- *a flat area*

There are no winners or losers in jump rope; you just take turns jumping with your friends. And to add to the fun, you can rhyme at the same time!

1 Two people hold the ends of the rope and swing it in an arc so that it just skims the ground on the downswing and reaches above the head of the jumper on the upswing.

2 A player jumps over the rope as it swings near the ground; she jumps until she misses or until another player wants a turn.

3 When your turn is over, try to jump out of the way while the rope is still swinging, but without letting it touch you. The next player steps up to the swinging rope and immediately starts jumping.

4 Players can keep track of the number of jumps they make by reciting this rhyme:

> *Cinderella, dressed in yellow,*
> *Went upstairs to kiss a fellow.*
> *By mistake she kissed a snake.*
> *How many doctors did it take?*
> *1, 2, 3, 4 . . .*

24

5 Players can also perform the actions in this rhyme as they jump:

Teddy Bear, Teddy Bear, turn around.

Teddy Bear, Teddy Bear, touch the ground.

Teddy Bear, Teddy Bear, shine your shoes.

Teddy Bear, Teddy Bear, read the news.

Teddy Bear, Teddy Bear, go upstairs.

Teddy Bear, Teddy Bear, say your prayers.

Teddy Bear, Teddy Bear, turn out the light.

Teddy Bear, Teddy Bear, say good night!

● **For more fun:** To make the game more challenging, the jumper can ask the rope swingers to turn the rope faster by saying "Hot peppers!" or higher by calling out "High waters!" To slow them down again, call out "Salt!" and to have them lower the rope, say "Low waters!"

25

HORSE

In this basketball game, if you miss a shot, you are in danger of becoming a horse.

1 Choose a player to go first. (See page 6.)

2 The first player tries to shoot a ball through the basketball hoop from anywhere on the court.

3 If he misses, then the next player can shoot from wherever she likes.

4 But if the first player makes the shot, then the next player must shoot from the exact same place.

5 If the second player makes the shot, she can shoot again from anywhere around the hoop, and the next player must follow her lead.

6 If the second player misses, she gets an "H," the first letter in the word "HORSE." Every time someone misses a shot that the player before her made, she gets a letter. A player who gets all five letters in "HORSE" is out of the game.

7 The game is over when all but one player, the winner, is out.

WHAT YOU NEED

- *2 or more players*
- *a basketball*
- *a basketball hoop*

26

sHaRKs & MINNOWs

See how fast you can swim as you pretend
to be a timid minnow or a hungry shark!

1 Divide the group into two teams, sharks and minnows. (See page 8.)

2 The sharks get in the water, and all the minnows stand at one end of the pool.

3 The minnows dive in and try to swim from one end of the pool to the other without being tagged by a shark. If a minnow is completely underwater, she is safe from being tagged.

4 If a minnow is tagged, she is out of the game. If she makes it to the other end of the pool, she earns a point for her team.

5 When the minnows have all made it to the other side of the pool or have been tagged, the teams switch and play again.

6 Whichever team has the most points wins.

● **Safety tip:** Don't play this game unless there is a lifeguard or another adult watching the pool.

WHAT YOU NEED

● *4 or more players*
● *a swimming pool (outdoor or indoor)*
● *an adult to supervise*

27

MARCO POLO

This swimming game is named for a great explorer who traveled all the way from Europe to China. You will swim far in this watery game of tag.

This swimming game is named for a great explorer who traveled all the way from Europe to China. You will swim far in this watery game of tag.

WHAT YOU NEED

WHAT YOU NEED

- *2 or more players*
- *a swimming pool (outdoor or indoor)*
- *an adult to supervise*

1 Choose one player to be *It*. (See page 6.)

2 *It* must keep his eyes closed and try to tag the other players swimming around him.

3 To find the other players, *It* can say "Marco," to which all the other players must respond "Polo." The players cannot swim with their heads underwater, because they must be able to hear and respond to *It* at all times.

4 When a player is tagged, he becomes *It*.

● **Safety tip:** Don't play this game unless there is a lifeguard or another adult watching the pool.

FREEZE TAG

**Can you stand perfectly still?
You'll find out when you play this game.**

WHAT YOU NEED

- *6 or more players*
- *a large area*

1 Divide the group into two teams and decide which team will be *It*. (See page 6 and page 8.)

2 The team that is *It* tries to tag the other players. Anyone who is tagged must freeze in place. (But players who haven't been tagged can unfreeze their teammates by touching them.)

3 The *It* team wins when they have frozen everyone.

● **For more fun:** There is a similar game called **TV TAG**. If a player calls out the name of a TV show and sits down just before he is tagged, he is safe and gets a chance to run away again.

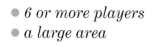

FLASHLIGHT TAG

This hiding game is fun to play on a dark night.

1 Pick an area or object to be home base. When someone is touching the base, he is safe and cannot be tagged.

2 Choose one person to be *It*. (See page 6.)

3 *It* closes her eyes and counts to one hundred while the other players hide.

4 Now *It* opens her eyes and searches for the other players, using the flashlight. When she shines her light on a player and calls his name, the player is "tagged" and is out of the game.

5 But if players sneak back to home base without being seen, they are safe.

6 The game is over when all of the players have been tagged or are safe on home base. The last person to be tagged is *It*. Or if *It* did not tag anyone, she is *It* again.

WHAT
YOU
NEED

- *4 or more players*
- *a flashlight*
- *a large area with good hiding places*

BECKONS WANTED

- *4 or more players*
- *a large area with lots of hiding places*

BUZZZZ!

Fill the evening with spooky sounds as you play this noisy game of hide-and-seek.

1 Choose someone to be *It*. (See page 6.) Then pick an object like a big tree or a back door to be home base. When players are touching the base, *It* can't tag them.

2 Now *It* counts to one hundred while standing next to home base. Everyone else hides.

3 When *It* is done counting, she shouts, "Ready or not, here I come. Beckons wanted!"

4 Everyone in hiding must now make a noise. Any loud sound is fine. Nighttime noises like the hoot of an owl or the screech of a bird add to the spookiness of the game.

RRROARR!

WOOF!

MAX

Screetch! Screeeeetch!

Beckons Wanted!

Tweet! Tweet!

5 Now *It* can follow the sounds to find and tag the hidden players. *It* can call "Beckons wanted!" as many times as she likes, and each time the hidden players must respond.

6 While *It* searches, the players try to get back to home base without being tagged.

7 The first person to be tagged is *It*. If everyone makes it back to home base without being tagged, *It* is *It* again. You can keep playing until it's time to go inside.

● **Helpful hint for IT:** You shouldn't say "Beckons wanted!" too many times, as the other players will then know where you are and you won't be able to sneak up on them.

● **Helpful hint for the hidden players:** If you all make lots of different types of sounds at the same time, *It* will have trouble picking out a single sound to follow.

GHOST IN THE GRAVEYARD

- - - - - - - - - - - - -

WHAT YOU NEED

- *4 or more players*
- *a large area with lots of hiding places*

It's best to play this spooky game in the evening, when it is hard to see someone creeping up on you.

1 Choose someone to be the ghost, or *It*. (See page 6.) Then pick an object, such as a mailbox, a street lamp, or a tree, to be home base. When players are touching the base, the ghost can't tag them.

2 The ghost hides while the other players close their eyes and count out the hours until midnight: "One o'clock, two o'clock, three o'clock, four o'clock . . . eleven o'clock, midnight!"

3 Now the players say, "Apples, peaches, pumpkin pie; if you're not ready, holler 'I'!"

4 If the ghost says she is not ready, then the players count to midnight again before starting to look for her.

5 The players search for the ghost. As they walk around, she tries to sneak up and tag one of them without any player spotting her. If she tags a player, he becomes the ghost for the next game.

6 But if any of the players spots her first, he can shout, "Ghost in the graveyard!" and all the players can try to get back to home base before the ghost tags them. If they do, then the ghost has to be the ghost again in the next game.

33

CRACK THE WHIP

**A human chain becomes a whip
in this running game. You'd better hold on tight!**

W H A T
Y O U
N E E D

- *6 or more players*
- *a soft, grassy area*

1 Everyone lines up side by side and holds hands. The largest, strongest person should stand at one end of the line. He will "crack" the whip.

2 All the players begin to run as fast as they can. When they have reached full speed, the large player at the end of the line stops running suddenly, holds tightly to the person next to him, and digs his heel into the ground.

3 This action will cause the other players to swing around him, and the ones at the other end of the whip may go flying off.

- **Safety tip:** This should be played on soft ground in case someone falls down.

- **For more fun:** This game can also be played on ice skates or roller skates, but be very careful!

TUG-OF-WAR

**This is a good game to play with a large group
of people. It will test your strength and patience.**

W H A T
Y O U
N E E D

- *8 or more players*
- *a rope*
- *chalk or a stick for marking*
- *a soft, grassy area*

1 Mark a line on the ground.

2 Divide the group into two teams. (See page 8.) Make sure that all the stronger people are not on the same team.

3 Each team holds an end of the rope and stands on either side of the line.

4 Now each team tugs on the rope, trying to pull the other team toward them and across the line.

5 The team that pulls *every* player on the other team across the line wins.

RED ROVER

**You can play this game with lots of friends,
but you have to be careful whom you invite over.**

1 Divide the group into two teams. (See page 8.)

2 The two teams stand facing each other with about twenty feet between them. The team members should stand side by side, holding hands firmly.

3 The teams take turns calling to each other, "Red Rover, Red Rover, send [the name of a member of the other team] right over!" That person comes running as fast as she can toward the team that called to her. If she breaks through the team's line, she gets to take a player back to join her team's line.

4 If she doesn't break through, she stays and joins the opposing team.

5 The game is over when one team has all the players. That team wins!

● *8 or more players*
● *a large area*

LeaPFROG

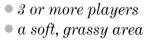

Have you ever wondered what it would be like to be a frog? You'll find out how to hop like one when you play this game.

- *3 or more players*
- *a soft, grassy area*

1 Line up, one player behind the other, leaving several feet between you and the player in front of you.

2 Everyone squats on the ground like a frog: bend your knees, sit on your heels, and place your hands on the ground in front of you.

3 The last player in line hops or takes a running leap toward the player in front of him, places his hands on the player's back, and leaps over him with his legs spread wide.

4 He leaps over all the players in the line until he reaches the front, and then he squats down again.

5 The new last person in line does the same thing. The game ends when everyone is tired!

● **For more fun:** You can divide the group into teams and have a Leapfrog race!

Indoor & Party Games

TELEPHONE

- *6 or more players*

Telephone, also known as "Gossip,"
is a goofy game for friends of all ages. Best of all,
it's easy to play anywhere, anytime.

1 Form a line.

2 The first person in line thinks of a secret message (a word, a phrase, or a sentence), whispers it to the second person, who then whispers it to the third person, and so on, until the last person in line has heard it. No repeating is allowed! Just pass on the message as you hear it, even if you are not sure you heard it correctly.

3 The last person in line then says the message out loud. It's probably not the same thing the first person said. And that's the fun of the game—to discover the difference between what's said and what's heard.

4 Start again, but this time let a new person go to the front of the line.

● **Here's an example:** The first person in line thinks to herself, "What a nice day," which she whispers to the second person in line. This person might hear "Lots of mice today," which he then whispers to the third person, who hears "Lost mice for sale." By the time the message finally reaches the last person, she might say out loud, "Posters of snails!" or something equally silly!

Because

Do you like making up stories? Here is your chance to tell one with the help of your friends.

● *3 or more players*

1 One player starts by describing an event. For example, the first player might say, "I woke up in the middle of the night . . ."

2 The next player continues the story by giving a reason for what happened. He begins with the word "because." He might say ". . . because I dreamed I was being chased by a giant peanut butter-and-jelly sandwich . . ."

3 And each player gives an explanation for what the previous person said. The sillier the reason, the better.

4 You can keep adding to the story for as long as you like, but try to give your explanations as quickly as possible.

39

MUSICAL CHAIRS

WHAT YOU NEED

- 6 or more players
- a CD or cassette player
- music CDs or audiocassettes
- someone to play the music
- a chair for each player but one

1 Line up two rows of chairs back-to-back. Be sure there is one chair fewer than there are players.

2 Ask someone who isn't playing to be in charge of the music. When she turns the music on, everyone walks around the chairs.

3 After a few minutes the music is turned off, and the players quickly try to sit down in the closest chair. The player who doesn't find a chair of his own is out of the game.

4 Take away one chair and start the music again. When it stops, everyone should scramble for a chair. The player without one is out, and the game goes on until there are just two players walking around one chair. Whoever sits in the chair first is the winner!

BUTTON, BUTTON, WHO'S GOT THE BUTTON?

See if you can find the button, but you have to look carefully, because your friends will try to trick you.

WHAT YOU NEED

● *5 or more players*
● *a button or other small object*

1 Choose one player to be *It*. (See page 6.) This player has the button.

2 All the players but *It* sit in a circle with their hands cupped behind their backs.

3 *It* walks around the circle and pretends to put the button in the hands of each player. Eventually, he actually does put the button in one player's hands, but he doesn't want anyone else to know who has it, so he might keep pretending to give it to other players.

4 The other players should watch carefully and try to figure out who received the button.

5 When he thinks he has fooled the other players, *It* goes to the middle of the circle and asks each player, "Button, button, who's got the button?"

6 The first player who guesses correctly is *It* for the next game.

● **Helpful hint:** While everyone is guessing, the person who actually has the button should say the name of another player to keep the others from knowing that he has it.

BUZZ

The room will sound as if it's full of bees when you play this crazy counting game.

W H A T
Y O U
N E E D

● *4 or more players*

1 Everyone sits in a circle. Someone starts counting. Each player calls out a number in turn, but when you reach the number 7, any number with 7 in it, or any number divisible by 7, you say "Buzz" instead of the number.

2 Your counting will sound like this: "1, 2, 3, 4, 5, 6, Buzz, 8, 9, 10, 11, 12, 13, Buzz, 15, 16, Buzz, 18, 19, 20, Buzz, 22, . . ." If you get to 71, you say "Buzz-one," and so on. The number 77 is "Buzz-buzz."

3 If a player forgets to say "Buzz" in place of the number, he is out of the game.

4 The game is over when only one person is left. She is the winner!

CONCENTRATION

You have to pay attention to stay in this game, but playing is a snap!

WHAT YOU NEED

● *4 or more players*

1 Sit in a circle and count off so that each player has a number.

2 Player number one starts the rhythm:

Hit your thighs with both hands.

Then clap your hands.

Snap the fingers of your right hand.

Then snap the fingers of your left hand.

3 Everyone joins in, repeating the moves of the first player over and over again.

4 When everyone has got the rhythm, the first player starts the game. As he snaps his right hand, he says his own number. Then, as he snaps his left hand, he says the number of another player. This person goes next, saying her own number as she snaps her right hand and someone else's number as she snaps her left hand, and so on.

5 Any player who loses the rhythm or misses his turn when his number is called is out of the game.

6 The game is over when only one player, the winner, is left.

43

BODIES

You know where your nose is, don't you? Well, this game might make you forget.

- *4 or more players*

1 Choose someone to be the leader. (See page 6.)

2 The leader stands in front of the rest of the group and begins the game by touching her ear and saying, "Ear, ear, ear . . ." The other players also touch their ears.

3 Then suddenly the leader names another body part, such as "nose," but this time she points to her forehead.

4 The other players must do what she *says*, not what she *does*. So they must touch their noses, not their foreheads. Any player who touches his forehead is out of the game.

5 The leader keeps trying to trick the other players into touching the wrong parts of their bodies until all but one player is out of the game. This last player gets to be the leader of the next game.

44

sardines

In this game of hide-and-seek, see how many friends can fit in one hiding place!

1 Pick someone to be *It*. (See page 6.)

2 *It* hides while the other players count to one hundred with their eyes closed.

3 Everyone searches for *It*. When a player finds *It*, he doesn't say anything. He quietly hides with *It*.

4 Each player who finds *It* squeezes into the hiding place, until there is only one player left looking.

5 The last player to find *It* becomes *It* in the next game.

MILK CAPS

Milk caps are colorful cardboard disks.
They were once used to seal milk bottles.
Now you can use them to play a fun game.

1 Choose one player to go first. You can decide by flipping a milk cap just as you would a coin. (See page 7.)

2 All the players put their milk caps in a big stack. The printed sides should be face up.

3 The first player takes his slammer and throws it at the stack, trying to hit the milk caps hard so they flip over. You can throw the slammer by holding the rim with your thumb and forefinger and tossing it down flat on top of the stack.

4 The player gets to keep the milk caps that he flips blank side up.

5 The rest of the caps are stacked up again, and the next player tries to flip them with her slammer.

6 The game is over when all of the milk caps have been flipped over. The winner is the person with the most milk caps.

- *2 or more players*
- *at least 4 milk caps*
- *1 milk-cap slammer (a thicker, heavier milk cap) for each player*

WASTEBASKET BASKETBALL

WHAT YOU NEED

- *1 or more players*
- *paper*
- *tape*
- *a wastepaper basket or a bucket*

This is a good game to play when you are alone or when it's too rainy to play basketball outside.

1 Make a ball by crumpling the paper and taping it into a small, round shape.

2 Stand ten feet away from the basket. Try to throw the paper ball into the basket.

3 You get two points each time you make a basket. Try to get to twenty points.

4 If you are playing with friends, everyone should take turns throwing the ball. The first person who gets to twenty points wins.

● **For more fun:** To make the game more challenging, each time you make a basket, try the next shot from a step farther away.

PIN THE TAIL ON THE DONKEY

**In this favorite party game,
players try to give the donkey a tail.**

1 Hang the picture of the donkey on the wall. Put some tape at the end of each tail-shaped piece.

2 Choose a player to go first. Tie the scarf around the player's head so she cannot see. Give her one of the tail-shaped pieces.

3 Now spin her around three times, point her in the direction of the donkey picture, and let her go.

4 The player tries to stick the tail on the end of the donkey. When she thinks she has put it in the right place, she can take the blindfold off to see how close her piece is.

5 Each player is blindfolded in turn and tries to put his tail-shaped piece on the end of the donkey.

6 After everyone has had a turn, the player who placed the tail closest to the end of the donkey wins the game!

- *4 or more players*
- *a large picture of a donkey without a tail*
- *a tail-shaped piece for each player*
- *some tape*
- *a scarf*

PIÑATA

There is candy for everyone at the end of this delicious party game.

1 Hang the piñata from the ceiling or from the branch of a tree. It should be just above the players' heads.

2 Choose someone to go first. (See page 6.) Tie the scarf around the first player's head so he cannot see. Give him the stick and spin him around several times.

3 Now the blindfolded player tries to hit the piñata hard enough to break it open. He can have three swings.

4 Everyone takes turns hitting the piñata until it breaks open and the candy spills out. All the players get to eat the candy!

● **Safety tip:** Everyone should stand away from the blindfolded player to avoid the swinging stick.

- *2 or more players*
- *a piñata (a papier-mâché figure filled with candy)*
- *a scarf*
- *a long stick or bat*

49

aPPLe BUBLING

For Halloween parties or anytime, here is a tricky game for apple lovers!

- *4 or more players*
- *an apple for each player*
- *a big basin or bucket full of water*

1 Float the apples in the water.

2 Choose a player to go first. (See page 6.) The player puts her hands behind her back and tries to pick up an apple using just her mouth, but she can't bite the stem!

3 She can keep trying until she gets an apple, and then it is the next player's turn. The game is over when everyone has an apple!

● **For more fun:** Tie more apples by the stem to pieces of string. There should be one for each player. Then hang the apples at face height from the ceiling or a door frame. All at the same time, the players try to bite the apples without using their hands. The first person to bite one wins!

PASS THE ORANGE

**W H A T
Y O U
N E E D**

**Giving an orange to a friend is easy, right?
Well, what if you can't use your hands?**

1 Divide the group into two teams. (See page 8.)

2 Each team lines up with players standing side by side.

3 The first person in each line takes an orange and holds it under his chin by pressing it against his chest. Keeping his hands behind his back, he passes the orange to the next person in his team as quickly as he can.

4 This person must take the orange with his chin, and without using his hands. He passes it on to the next player in line.

5 If the orange drops, then the first person in line must pick it up, put it under his chin, and start passing it again.

6 The first team to pass the orange all the way to the end of the line wins!

- *10 or more players*
- *2 oranges*

BALLOON RELAY RACE

- *6 or more players*
- *string*
- *2 balloons*
- *2 square pieces of cardboard*
- *a large space cleared of furniture*

In this relay game, you have to keep the balloon in the air if you want to move forward.

1 Divide the group into two teams. (See page 8.)

2 Mark a starting line at one end of the room with a piece of string.

3 The two teams line up behind the string.

4 One player from each team takes a balloon and a piece of cardboard. The two players fan the balloons with the cardboard so that the balloons stay in the air.

5 Now the players must race each other across the room and back, keeping the balloons in the air in front of them. They cannot hit the balloons with the cardboard. If a player lets the balloon drop, he must go back to the starting line and begin again.

6 When they make it back to the line, the players pass the cardboard to the next teammate without letting the balloons drop.

7 Their teammates must now fan the balloons across the room and back, too.

8 The first team to complete the race wins.

Car Games

FIND THE ALPHABET

**The alphabet is all around you.
See how quickly you can find it on a car trip.**

- *1 or more players*

1 Look out the car window at the signs and license plates that you pass and see if you can find the letter "A." When you have found that, look for the letter "B," and continue looking for each letter of the alphabet until you've reached the end. You can time yourself.

2 If you are playing with other people, then the first person to see a letter calls it out and describes where he has seen it: "I see the letter 'C' on that California license plate." The other players must look for the letter someplace else.

3 The winner is the first person to get to the end of the alphabet.

FIFTY STATES

This game is great for long car trips and is a good way to remember the names of all the states.

- *1 or more players*
- *a pencil*
- *paper*

1 Look out the car window at the license plates of the other cars you see. Each state has its own distinctive license plate. Write down the state names you spot.

2 See how many of the fifty states you can find on your trip.

● **For more fun:** Try to remember the capital and state flower or bird of each state you spot. Sometimes the license plates will have a picture of the state flower or bird on them.

GRANDMOTHER'S TRUNK

● *2 or more players*

**Some people like to pack a lot
of stuff. See how many silly things
you can think of to put in a trunk.**

1 Someone starts by naming one item that Grandmother might pack in her trunk: "Grandmother packed an igloo."

2 The next player repeats that item and then thinks of another beginning with the same letter: "Grandmother packed an igloo and an inchworm."

3 Players take turns adding to the list, but with each new item they must repeat the previous items mentioned in order, without leaving any out.

4 If a player makes a mistake, he is out of the game. The winner is the last person left in the game.

HINKY PINKY

● *2 or more players*

**If you like to make up rhymes,
this game will test your skills!**

1 One player thinks of two words that rhyme—like "fickle pickle"—but she doesn't say them aloud. Instead she tells the other players how many syllables they have by saying one of the following:

"hink pink" for words with one syllable each;
"hinky pinky" for words with two syllables each;
"hinkety pinkety" for words with three syllables each.

2 She also gives the other players a brief description of what her words mean. For instance, she might say, "I'm thinking of a hinky pinky that means a choosy gherkin." The first person to guess "fickle pickle" gets to think of the next rhyme.

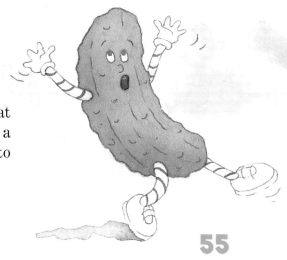

TWE TY QUE TI

● *2 or more players*

In this guessing game, you may ask a lot of questions, but the answer could be anything!

1 One player thinks of a person or thing and tells the other players if it is animal, vegetable, or mineral.

2 Now the other players take turns asking questions about it that can be answered "yes" or "no." But they can ask only twenty questions. The person who asks the question that reveals the answer gets to think of the next animal, vegetable, or mineral.

● **Helpful hints:** Remember that an animal can be a pig, a worm, or even a human who is alive, dead, or fictional. The animal category also includes anything derived from an animal, such as leather, silk, milk, and so on. The vegetable category includes not only plants but things made from plants, such as paper or peanut butter. And minerals are everything else. Also, the broader the questions you begin with, the more information you can get with the answer. For instance, if you are trying to think of an animal, you can ask, "Is it a human being?" If the answer is yes, then you don't have to ask questions about any other animal.

Singing
Games

I'M a LITTLE TEAPOT

Can you pretend to be a teapot? If you follow
the pictures as you sing this song, you will soon look like one.

I'm a lit - tle tea - pot, short and stout. Here is my

han - dle, here is my spout. When I start to steam up,

then I shout: Tip me o - ver and pour me out.

DO YOUR EARS HANG LOW?

Nobody has ears this long, but this song shows all the fun things you could do with them if you did! Follow the motions as you sing.

Do your ears hang low? Do they wob-ble to and fro? Can you tie them in a knot? Can you tie them in a bow? Can you throw them o-ver your shoul-der like a con-ti-nen-tal sol-dier? Do your ears hang low?

● **For more fun:** See how fast you can sing this song and still do the motions.

Head & Shoulders, Knees & Toes!

This game will keep you on your toes! As you sing,
point to the part of your body named in the song.

Head and shoul-ders, knees and toes, knees and toes!   Head and shoul-ders, knees and

toes, knees and toes!_____   Eyes and ears and mouth— and— nose!

Head   and shoul - ders, knees and   toes,   knees   and toes!

● **For more fun:** Now sing the song again several times, each time a little faster. See how
quickly you can sing it and still point to the right part of your body!

THE eLePHaNT SONG

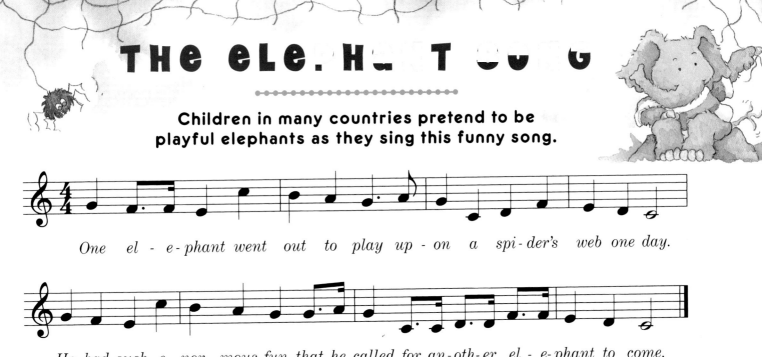

Children in many countries pretend to be playful elephants as they sing this funny song.

One el - e-phant went out to play up - on a spi-der's web one day.

He had such e - nor - mous fun that he called for an-oth-er el - e-phant to come.

VERSE 2
Two elephants went out to play
Upon a spider's web one day.
They had such enormous fun
That they called for another elephant to come.

1 Everyone stands in a circle and sings the song.

2 As you sing the first verse, one player walks like an elephant around the inside of the circle, moving slowly and swaying back and forth. He holds one arm stretched out in front of his nose like a trunk and the other behind him like a tail.

3 As you sing the second verse, the first player chooses someone to join him inside the circle. This player holds the "tail" of the first player in his "trunk."

4 You can keep singing and playing until everyone has joined the line of elephants.

61

LONDON BRIDGE

If you don't want the bridge to fall on you,
you'd better move quickly to the music.

Lon - don Bridge is fall - ing down, fall - ing down, fall - ing down.

Lon - don Bridge is fall - ing down, my fair la - dy.

VERSE 2
Build it up with sticks and stones,
Sticks and stones, sticks and stones.
Build it up with sticks and stones,
My fair lady.

VERSE 3
Sticks and stones will fall away,
Fall away, fall away.
Sticks and stones will fall away,
My fair lady.

VERSE 4
Shake her up with pepper and salt,
Pepper and salt, pepper and salt.
Shake her up with pepper and salt,
My fair lady.

VERSE 5
Take a key and lock her up,
Lock her up, lock her up.
Take a key and lock her up,
My fair lady.

1 Two players stand facing each other with their hands clasped together and their arms raised over their heads, forming a "bridge" for the other players to walk under.

2 As everyone sings the first three verses of the song, other players take turns walking under the arms.

3 At the words "My fair lady" at the end of the third verse ("Sticks and stones will fall away . . ."), the two players drop their arms, trying to catch a player in between.

4 As the fourth verse is sung, they shake the captured player back and forth. And then, with the fifth verse, they lead her over to a spot away from the game. This is the "jail."

5 The game continues until everyone is captured. The last two prisoners get to be the "bridge" in the next game.

JAIL

Index